BEST OF DINER CLASSICS

GARDEN *of* GRAPES.

First Edition: 2023

Published by Garden of Grapes.

Printed in USA

The recipes, techniques, and tips in this cookbook are intended for personal use only. The author and publisher are not responsible for any adverse effects or consequences resulting from the use of the recipes or suggestions in this book.

Library of Congress Cataloging-in-Publication Data:

First edition.
Includes index.

Manufactured in USA

Introduction

In the world of diners, where chrome gleams, and the promise of comfort food lingers in the air, I extend a hearty welcome. I'm not just your guide through these pages; consider me your diner companion, a culinary comrade on this journey down memory lane.

The Theme Unveiled: A Taste of Nostalgia

Now, you might wonder, why diner classics? Well, my friends, diners are more than eateries; they are cultural landmarks, time capsules of flavors that transport us to simpler times. This cookbook is a homage to those cherished diner moments, a ticket to relive the tastes that linger in our memories like a favorite tune.

Inspiration Behind the Grill: A Culinary Time Machine

What inspired this culinary endeavor? It's the sizzle of a grill, the aroma of coffee brewing, and the symphony of flavors that dance on a diner plate. It's the nostalgia that accompanies a bite of a perfectly cooked burger or a forkful of creamy mac 'n' cheese. These diners, with their checkered floors and neon signs, are the backdrop to countless stories, and I wanted to capture that essence.

What Awaits You: An Overview of the Feast

Within these pages, you'll find more than recipes; you'll find a passport to the heart of American diner cuisine. From crispy fried chicken that rivals grandma's secret recipe to fluffy pancakes that practically whisper "Sunday morning," each page holds a culinary revelation. Get ready for a culinary road trip, exploring 100+ recipes that pay homage to the classics—those dishes that have stood the test of time and continue to bring comfort to our tables.

So, my fellow diners of the digital age, buckle up. We're embarking on a journey through taste and time. Let the clinking of forks, the sizzle of griddles, and the warmth of nostalgia guide you through the "Best of Diner Classics Cookbook." Here's to good eats and even better memories. Enjoy the feast!

Cooking Philosophy or Approach

Cooking Philosophy or Approach: A Taste of Nostalgia

Welcome to the world of diner classics—a realm where comfort, flavor, and a touch of nostalgia collide on the plate. In this cookbook, we embark on a culinary journey that pays homage to the timeless American diners, where every dish tells a story of shared meals, laughter, and a love for simple, yet extraordinary, flavors.

Philosophy: Honoring the Tradition

Cooking, to me, is not just about creating a meal; it's a celebration of tradition. In this cookbook, you'll find a deep respect for the classic American diner fare that has comforted generations. The philosophy is rooted in preserving the essence of these dishes while infusing a contemporary touch to suit modern palates.

Approach: Flavorful Simplicity

My approach to cooking is all about balancing simplicity and flavor. The recipes in this collection are a testament to the idea that a few high-quality ingredients, prepared with care, can result in dishes that are not only satisfying but downright unforgettable. It's about letting the flavors shine without unnecessary complications.

Techniques: Mastering the Basics

While we explore the realm of diner classics, the emphasis is on mastering the basics. From the perfect burger patty to the flakiest pie crust, the techniques highlighted in this cookbook are the building blocks of American diner cuisine. It's a guide to achieving that ideal balance of textures and flavors that define these beloved dishes.

Ingredients: Quality First

In the world of diner classics, the quality of ingredients takes center stage. Whether it's the juiciest tomatoes for a classic BLT or the richest beef for a hearty meatloaf, the emphasis is on sourcing ingredients that elevate the dish. The cookbook encourages a mindful approach to ingredient selection, respecting the integrity of each component.

Style: Approachable Elegance

The style of this cookbook is rooted in approachable elegance. While we celebrate the down-to-earth nature of diner classics, there's a touch of refinement in the presentation and preparation. It's about bringing a bit of sophistication to the diner table without losing the essence of what makes these dishes truly comforting.

So, fellow food enthusiasts, as you embark on this culinary journey through the "Best of Diner Classics Cookbook," know that each recipe is a nod to the rich tapestry of American diner culture. It's an invitation to savor the flavors of nostalgia while appreciating the beauty of simplicity in every bite. Get ready to relive the magic of diner dining in your own kitchen!

Tips for Successful Cooking

Welcome to the heart of the diner classics experience. In this section, we're not just throwing ingredients together; we're orchestrating a symphony of flavors that harken back to the golden era of American diners. Here are some tips to ensure your culinary journey through the "Best of Diner Classics Cookbook" is a taste of pure nostalgia:

1. Quality Ingredients are Key:
   - In the world of diner classics, the quality of your ingredients is paramount. Opt for fresh, locally sourced produce, and don't skimp on the basics like butter, eggs, and flour. The classics deserve the best.

2. Embrace Simplicity:
   - Diner classics are about hearty, uncomplicated goodness. Keep it simple; let the flavors shine. A well-seasoned steak needs little more than a hot grill and a sprinkle of salt and pepper.

3. Perfect Your Pancake Flip:
   - Ah, the elusive perfect pancake flip. The secret? A hot griddle, a patient wrist, and the confidence to let it cook undisturbed until bubbles form. Then, with a swift motion, flip and let the other side dance in the golden glow.

4. Master the Art of the Over-Easy Egg:
   - Achieving the perfect over-easy egg is an art form. The key is a hot, non-stick skillet, a gentle touch, and the finesse to flip without breaking the yolk. It's a dance; don't rush it.

5. Build Flavor with the Maillard Reaction:
   - The Maillard reaction is your ally. Whether it's the sear on a burger or the crispness of bacon, let that beautiful browning add layers of flavor to your diner creations.

6. Don't Fear the Deep Fryer:

- Some classics demand a plunge into hot oil. Embrace the deep fryer for crispy fries, onion rings, or the iconic fried chicken. Just remember, patience is a virtue when achieving that golden perfection.

7. Be Bold with Sauces and Condiments:

- Diner classics often come with a signature sauce or condiment. Experiment with homemade ketchup, secret sauce, or a tangy relish. It's the finishing touch that elevates the dish.

8. Get to Know Your Grill:

- Whether it's for a juicy burger or a perfectly grilled cheese sandwich, the grill is a diner's best friend. Learn to control the heat, master the grill marks, and let the smoky essence infuse your classics.

Remember, these tips are your ticket to recreating the magic of classic American diners in your own kitchen. So, put on your apron, channel your inner diner chef, and let the nostalgia-infused cooking adventure begin!

Kitchen Essentials

Welcome to the heart of your culinary adventure, where the clatter of pots and pans is the symphony of creation. In the spirit of mastering the "Best of Diner Classics Cookbook: A Taste of Nostalgia - 100+ Best Copycat Classic American Dinners Recipes," let's talk about the tools that will turn your kitchen into a haven of delicious nostalgia.

1. The Trusty Cast-Iron Skillet:
   - This isn't just a piece of cookware; it's a culinary workhorse. From searing steaks to crafting the perfect cornbread, the cast-iron skillet is your partner in crime.

2. Sharp Chef's Knife:
   - A chef's knife is not just a tool; it's an extension of your hand. Keep it sharp, and it'll slice through onions, tomatoes, and memories of diners past like a breeze.

3. The Immersion Blender:
   - Say goodbye to lumpy soups and hello to silky perfection. The immersion blender is your secret weapon for achieving that diner-quality smoothness in your sauces and soups.

4. Stainless Steel Mixing Bowls:
   - Versatility is the name of the game. Whether you're whipping up pancake batter or tossing a fresh salad, these bowls are the unsung heroes of your kitchen.

5. Classic Diner Coffee Pot:
   - Because no diner experience is complete without a cup of Joe. Channel that nostalgia with a simple, no-frills coffee pot that delivers that familiar aroma.

6. Non-Stick Griddle:
   - Perfect for flipping pancakes, searing burgers, or griddling up a classic diner breakfast. Your go-to for achieving that golden brown perfection.

7. Wooden Spoon and Spatula Duo:
   - These aren't just utensils; they're the conductor's baton in your culinary orchestra. Gentle on your cookware and perfect for stirring, flipping, and sautéing.

8. Quality Baking Sheets:
   - From golden-brown cookies to crispy oven-fried chicken, a good baking sheet is the canvas for your culinary artistry.

Tips on How to Use These Tools Effectively:

   - Keep your cast-iron skillet seasoned for a natural non-stick surface.
   - Hone your knife skills; a sharp knife is a safe knife.
   - Invest in a quality chef's knife; it's a game-changer.
   - When using the immersion blender, immerse it fully for the smoothest results.
   - Preheat your stainless steel mixing bowls for easier dough handling.
   - Embrace the simplicity of the classic diner coffee pot; no need for fancy gadgets.
   - Season your griddle regularly to prevent sticking and ensure even cooking.
   - Wooden spoons and spatulas are your kitchen allies; treat them with care.
   - Invest in quality baking sheets with even heat distribution for consistent results.

Remember, these tools are not just instruments; they're extensions of your culinary passion. Master them, and you'll be well on your way to recreating the magic of classic American diners in the comfort of your own kitchen. Happy cooking, and may your diner classics be as comforting and nostalgic as the originals!

Flavor Pairing Suggestions

In the realm of diner classics, where every dish is a trip down memory lane, the art of flavor pairing is as crucial as the sizzle on the grill. Here are some suggestions to inspire your culinary adventures:

1. The Harmony of Sweet and Savory:
   - Classic diners have always celebrated the marriage of sweet and savory. Picture a stack of pancakes drizzled with maple syrup alongside crispy bacon. The sweetness balances the saltiness, creating a culinary duet that's as timeless as the diner itself.

2. Tomato and Basil Waltz:
   - Tomatoes and basil—two ingredients that dance together like old friends. Whether in a caprese salad or atop a juicy burger, their combination is a melody of freshness that resonates through diner classics.

3. Mustard and Pickles:
   - The tangy zip of mustard paired with the crunch of pickles—this dynamic duo is a staple in classic diner burgers and sandwiches. It's a flavor pairing that adds a zesty kick to every bite.

4. Garlic and Butter Ballet:
   - Garlic and butter waltz together in many diner classics, from garlic butter shrimp to garlic bread. This pairing elevates the richness of dishes, creating a luxurious dance on the taste buds.

5. The All-American Duo: Ketchup and Mayo:
   - Individually, ketchup and mayo are condiment royalty. Together, they form the backbone of countless diner sauces, from the classic burger spread to the beloved thousand island dressing.

6. Cinnamon and Nutmeg Symphony:

   - For a taste of nostalgia, embrace the warmth of cinnamon and nutmeg. These spices, whether in a classic apple pie or a warm bowl of oatmeal, create a comforting melody of fall flavors.

7. Chocolate and Coffee Encore:

   - The timeless combination of chocolate and coffee takes center stage in diners across America. Whether in a chocolate cake or a mocha milkshake, this pairing is a sweet, caffeinated symphony.

8. Cheddar and Bacon Rhapsody:

   - Cheddar and bacon—a duo that needs no introduction. From loaded baked potatoes to cheese-covered burgers, their partnership is a savory chorus that sings the praises of diner classics.

Feel free to let these suggestions inspire your culinary compositions. The diner kitchen is your stage, and the flavors are your instruments. Mix, match, and create your own nostalgic melodies, weaving the rich tapestry of classic American diner cuisine. Happy cooking!

INDEX

Chapter 1:
Breakfast Bonanza

4 pancakes   350   15

Fluffy Pancakes with Maple Syrup

These fluffy pancakes are a morning delight! They became popular during the Great Depression for their affordability and taste.

Ingredients:

- 1 cup all-purpose flour
- 2 tbsp sugar
- 2 tsp baking powder
- 1/2 tsp salt
- 1 cup milk
- 1 egg
- 2 tbsp melted butter

Directions

1. In a bowl, mix flour, sugar, baking powder, and salt.
2. In another bowl, whisk milk, egg, and melted butter.
3. Combine wet and dry ingredients.
4. Cook on a griddle until golden.

Fun Facts

Pancakes are older than you think, dating back to ancient Greece.
They were served with honey and wine!

2 eggs, 4
bacon strips

320

10

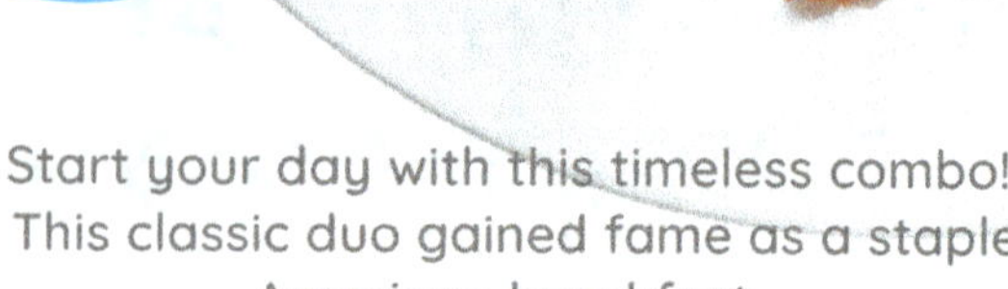

Classic Eggs and Bacon

Start your day with this timeless combo!
This classic duo gained fame as a staple
American breakfast.

Ingredients:

- 2 large eggs
- 4 bacon strips
- Salt and pepper to taste

Directions

1. Heat a skillet over medium heat.
2. Add bacon and cook until crisp.
3. Remove bacon and fry eggs in bacon grease.
4. Season and serve.

Fun Facts

Eggs Benedict was named after a Wall Street broker who wanted a new dish to cure his hangover.

2 biscuits, 1 cup gravy

450

30

Homestyle Biscuits and Gravy

A hearty Southern classic, biscuits smothered in creamy sausage gravy.
Its roots trace back to the American South.

Ingredients:

- 2 biscuits
- 1 lb pork sausage
- 1/4 cup flour
- 2 cups milk
- Salt and pepper to taste

Directions

1. Bake biscuits.
2. Cook sausage until brown.
3. Stir in flour and cook.
4. Add milk, stir until thick.
5. Season and pour over biscuits.

Fun Facts

Biscuits and Gravy was a staple for Confederate soldiers during the Civil War.

1 omelette   420   20

Denver Omelette

A Western omelette filled with ham, bell peppers, and cheese.
It was named after Denver, Colorado.

Ingredients:

- 3 large eggs
- 2 tbsp butter
- 1/4 cup diced ham
- 1/4 cup diced bell peppers
- 1/4 cup shredded cheddar cheese

Directions

1. Whisk eggs in a bowl.
2. Melt butter in a skillet.
3. Add ham and peppers, cook.
4. Pour eggs and top with cheese.
5. Fold and serve.

Fun Facts

The Denver omelette was created in the 19th century by Chinese immigrants in Colorado.

2 waffles   280   25

Buttermilk Waffles

Crispy on the outside, tender on the inside, and perfect with toppings.
Waffles date back to medieval Europe.

Ingredients:

- 1 1/2 cups all-purpose flour
- 2 tbsp sugar
- 1 1/2 tsp baking powder
- 1/2 tsp baking soda
- 1/2 tsp salt
- 2 large eggs
- 1 3/4 cups buttermilk
- 1/2 cup melted butter

Directions

1. Mix dry ingredients in a bowl.
2. In another bowl, whisk eggs, buttermilk, and melted butter.
3. Combine wet and dry ingredients.
4. Cook in a waffle iron.

Fun Facts

The first waffle irons were made of two metal plates with wooden handles, designed to cook waffles over an open flame.

2 servings   380   40

Corned Beef Hash

A savory blend of corned beef, potatoes, and onions, often served with eggs.
It gained fame during World War II.

Ingredients:

- 2 cups cooked corned beef, diced
- 2 cups diced potatoes
- 1/2 cup diced onions
- Salt and pepper to taste

Directions

1. Cook potatoes in a skillet until brown.
2. Add onions and cook.
3. Stir in corned beef, season.
4. Serve with eggs if desired.

Fun Facts

Corned Beef Hash was a popular ration during World War II due to its long shelf life.

4 pancakes   320   20

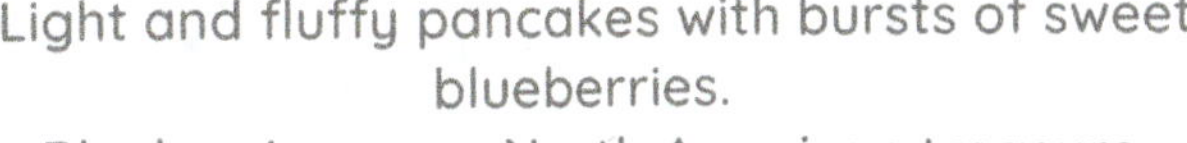

Blueberry Pancakes

Light and fluffy pancakes with bursts of sweet blueberries.
Blueberries are a North American treasure.

Ingredients:

- 1 cup all-purpose flour
- 2 tbsp sugar
- 2 tsp baking powder
- 1/2 tsp salt
- 1 cup milk
- 1 egg
- 2 tbsp melted butter
- 1/2 cup fresh blueberries

Directions

1. Mix flour, sugar, baking powder, and salt.
2. Whisk milk, egg, melted butter.
3. Combine wet and dry ingredients.
4. Add blueberries.
5. Cook on a griddle.

Fun Facts

Blueberries were used by Native Americans for their medicinal and culinary properties.

4 slices | 280 | 15

Cinnamon French Toast

Slices of bread soaked in a cinnamon-spiced egg mixture and cooked to perfection. French toast dates back to the Roman Empire.

Ingredients:

- 4 slices of bread
- 2 large eggs
- 1/2 cup milk
- 1/2 tsp ground cinnamon
- 1/4 tsp vanilla extract

Directions

1. Whisk eggs, milk, cinnamon, and vanilla.
2. Dip bread in the mixture.
3. Cook on a griddle until golden.

Fun Facts

The earliest reference to French toast is found in a Latin recipe dating back to the 4th or 5th century.

1 serving   550   35

Country Fried Steak and Eggs

A Southern favorite, breaded steak served with creamy gravy and eggs.
A comfort food from the heart of the South.

Ingredients:

- 1 country-fried steak
- 2 large eggs
- 1/2 cup milk
- Salt and pepper to taste

Directions

1. Cook the country-fried steak until golden.
2. In a separate pan, fry eggs.
3. Warm milk, season, and serve over steak.

Fun Facts

Country Fried Steak originated in Texas and was popularized during the Great Depression.

2 servings | 340 | 25

Huevos Rancheros

A Mexican breakfast dish with fried eggs on corn tortillas, smothered in tomato-chili sauce. A flavorful tradition from Mexico.

Ingredients:

- 4 corn tortillas
- 4 large eggs
- 1 cup tomato-chili sauce
- 1/2 cup black beans
- 1/4 cup crumbled queso fresco
- 2 tbsp chopped cilantro

Directions

1. Warm tortillas.
2. Fry eggs.
3. Heat sauce and beans.
4. Assemble with eggs, sauce, beans, cheese, and cilantro.

Fun Facts

Huevos Rancheros is a popular breakfast choice in Mexico and often enjoyed with a side of refried beans.

Chapter 2:
Burger Bliss

1 Burger

500

20 minutes

Classic Cheeseburger

An American classic, the cheeseburger is a symbol of simple culinary perfection. It became popular in the 1920s and remains a beloved favorite.

Ingredients:

- 1/2 lb ground beef
- 1 hamburger bun
- 1 slice of American cheese
- Lettuce, tomato, onion, pickles
- Ketchup and mustard

Directions

1. Preheat grill to medium-high heat.
2. Form ground beef into a patty, season with salt and pepper.
3. Grill patty for 4-5 minutes per side.
4. Toast the bun.
5. Assemble the burger with cheese and toppings.
6. Enjoy!

Fun Facts

Did you know the first cheeseburger was served at the Rite Spot restaurant in Pasadena, California, in 1924?

1 Burger 750 25 minutes

Bacon Double Cheeseburger

This indulgent burger features double the beef and crispy bacon, a mouthwatering delight for burger enthusiasts.

Ingredients:

- 2/3 lb ground beef
- 2 hamburger buns
- 4 slices of bacon
- 2 slices of American cheese
- Lettuce, tomato, onion
- Ketchup and mayonnaise

Directions

1. Cook bacon until crispy.
2. Form beef into two patties, season.
3. Grill patties for 4-5 minutes per side.
4. Toast buns.
5. Assemble with cheese, bacon, and toppings.
6. Savor the flavor!

Fun Facts

Bacon was first added to burgers in the 1920s, creating a sensation among burger lovers.

1 Burger

550

30 minutes

Mushroom Swiss Burger

A sophisticated twist on the classic, this burger features sautéed mushrooms and creamy Swiss cheese, a culinary masterpiece.

Ingredients:

- 1/2 lb ground beef
- 1 hamburger bun
- 1/2 cup sliced mushrooms
- 2 slices Swiss cheese
- Butter
- Onions
- Garlic
- Worcestershire sauce

Directions

1. Sauté mushrooms in butter until tender.
2. Form beef into a patty, season.
3. Grill patty for 4-5 minutes per side.
4. Toast bun.
5. Assemble with cheese and mushrooms.
6. Delight in the fusion of flavors.

Fun Facts

The mushroom Swiss burger gained popularity in the 1940s as a gourmet burger option.

1 Burger   600   35 minutes

BBQ Bacon Burger

Tangy barbecue sauce and crispy bacon elevate this burger to a whole new level of deliciousness.

Ingredients:

- 1/2 lb ground beef
- 1 hamburger bun
- 2 slices of bacon
- BBQ sauce
- Cheddar cheese
- Onions
- Pickles

Directions

1. Cook bacon until crispy.
2. Form beef into a patty, season.
3. Grill patty for 4-5 minutes per side.
4. Toast bun.
5. Top with cheese, bacon, and BBQ sauce.
6. Devour with relish.

Fun Facts

The BBQ bacon burger was first introduced in Texas in the 1950s, celebrating the region's love for barbecue flavors.

1 Burger   400   40 minutes

Veggie Burger with Avocado

A healthier alternative, this veggie burger features a patty made from plant-based ingredients and creamy avocado.

Ingredients:

- 1 veggie burger patty
- 1 whole-grain bun
- 1/2 avocado
- Lettuce
- Tomato
- Onion
- Mustard
- Vegan mayo

Directions

1. Grill veggie patty for 5 minutes on each side.
2. Mash avocado and spread on the bun.
3. Assemble with veggies and condiments.
4. Savor the wholesome goodness.

Fun Facts

The veggie burger gained popularity in the 1980s as people embraced vegetarian and vegan lifestyles.

1 Burger | 600 | 25 minutes

Patty Melt with Rye Bread

This burger combines the flavors of a classic patty melt with the rye bread, creating a delicious and comforting meal.

Ingredients:

- 1/2 lb ground beef
- 2 slices of rye bread
- 2 slices Swiss cheese
- Onions
- Butter
- Mustard
- Pickles

Directions

1. Sauté onions in butter until caramelized.
2. Form beef into a patty, season.
3. Grill patty for 4-5 minutes per side.
4. Toast rye bread.
5. Assemble with cheese and onions.
6. Enjoy this comforting delight.

Fun Facts

The patty melt was a popular diner item in the 1940s, known for its satisfying and homey flavors.

1 Burger   700   30 minutes

Western Bacon Cheeseburger

A taste of the Wild West, this burger features barbecue sauce, onion rings, and cheddar cheese for a flavor explosion.

Ingredients:

- 1/2 lb ground beef
- 1 hamburger bun
- 2 slices of bacon
- BBQ sauce
- Cheddar cheese
- Onion rings

Directions

1. Cook bacon until crispy.
2. Form beef into a patty, season.
3. Grill patty for 4-5 minutes per side.
4. Toast bun.
5. Assemble with cheese, bacon, BBQ sauce, and onion rings.
6. Yeehaw, it's a wild ride for your taste buds!

Fun Facts

The Western bacon cheeseburger was popularized by a famous fast-food chain in the 1980s.

1 Burger

650

40 minutes

Jalapeño Popper Burger

This spicy delight combines the flavors of jalapeño poppers with a juicy burger, a fiery treat for the adventurous palate.

Ingredients:

- 1/2 lb ground beef
- 1 hamburger bun
- 4 jalapeño peppers
- Cream cheese
- Bacon
- Lettuce
- Tomato
- Mayo

Directions

1. Roast jalapeño peppers until skin is blistered, then peel and seed.
2. Form beef into a patty, season.
3. Grill patty for 4-5 minutes per side.
4. Toast bun.
5. Assemble with cream cheese, bacon, and jalapeños.
6. Get ready for a spicy explosion!

Fun Facts

The jalapeño popper burger gained popularity in the 1990s as spicy foods became a culinary trend.

1 Burger   700   35 minutes

Philly Cheesesteak Burger

A twist on the Philly classic, this burger features thinly sliced steak, sautéed onions, and melted provolone cheese.

Ingredients:

- - 1/2 lb thinly sliced steak
- - 1 hamburger bun
- - 2 slices provolone cheese
- - Onions
- - Bell peppers
- - Worcestershire sauce

Directions

1. Sauté onions and bell peppers until tender.
2. Grill steak for 2-3 minutes per side.
3. Toast bun.
4. Assemble with cheese, steak, onions, and peppers.
5. Enjoy a taste of Philadelphia in a burger!

Fun Facts

The Philly cheesesteak burger was created in the 1970s, combining the flavors of the iconic Philly sandwich with a burger.

1 Burger

600

30 minutes

Normal

This burger is for the bold, featuring blackened seasoning and tangy blue cheese, a flavor explosion in every bite.

Black and Blue Burger

Ingredients:

- 1/2 lb ground beef
- 1 hamburger bun
- Blackening seasoning
- Blue cheese
- Lettuce
- Tomato
- Onion
- Mayo

Directions

1. Season beef with blackening seasoning.
2. Grill patty for 4-5 minutes per side.
3. Toast bun.
4. Assemble with blue cheese and toppings.
5. Get ready for a bold and flavorful experience!

Fun Facts

The black and blue burger was inspired by the blackened fish and blue cheese dishes, becoming popular in the 1990s.

Chapter 3:
Satisfying Sandwiches

1 sandwich | 700 | 20

Reuben Sandwich

A hearty sandwich with corned beef, sauerkraut, Swiss cheese, and Russian dressing.
A classic deli favorite.

Ingredients:

- 2 slices rye bread
- 4 oz corned beef
- 1/2 cup sauerkraut
- 2 slices Swiss cheese
- 2 tbsp Russian dressing

Directions

1. Spread Russian dressing on bread slices.
2. Layer corned beef, sauerkraut, and cheese.
3. Grill until cheese is melted.

Fun Facts

The Reuben sandwich was created in Omaha, Nebraska, in the early 20th century.

1 sandwich   550   15

Turkey Club with Avocado

A triple-decker delight with turkey, bacon, lettuce, tomato, and creamy avocado. A modern twist on a classic.

Ingredients:

- 3 slices toasted white bread
- 4 oz turkey
- 2 strips crispy bacon
- Lettuce and tomato
- 1/2 ripe avocado

Directions

1. Layer turkey, bacon, lettuce, tomato, and avocado between slices of bread.
2. Secure with toothpicks.

Fun Facts

The Turkey Club was popularized in the early 20th century at social clubs.

1 sandwich | 450 | 15

BLT with Crispy Bacon

A timeless favorite featuring crispy bacon, fresh lettuce, and ripe tomatoes. Simplicity at its best.

Ingredients:

- 2 slices toasted white bread
- 4 strips crispy bacon
- Lettuce and tomato
- Mayonnaise

Directions

1. Spread mayonnaise on bread slices.
2. Layer bacon, lettuce, and tomato.
3. Assemble into a sandwich.

Fun Facts

The BLT became popular in the early 20th century when supermarkets started selling pre-packaged bacon.

1 sandwich,
1 cup soup

480

20

Grilled Cheese and Tomato Soup

The ultimate comfort combo: gooey grilled cheese with a side of creamy tomato soup. A beloved childhood classic.

Ingredients:

- 2 slices white bread
- 2 slices cheddar cheese
- 2 tbsp butter
- 1 cup tomato soup

Directions

1. Butter one side of each bread slice.
2. Place cheese between slices (butter side out).
3. Grill until golden.
4. Serve with tomato soup.

Fun Facts

Grilled cheese sandwiches were a staple during the Great Depression due to their affordability.

1 sandwich   650   25

A decadent ham and cheese sandwich dipped
in egg and fried to perfection.
A French-inspired delight.

Monte Cristo

Ingredients:

- 2 slices white bread
- 2 oz ham
- 2 slices Swiss cheese
- 2 slices turkey
- 2 eggs
- 1/4 cup milk

Directions

1. Layer ham, cheese, and turkey between bread slices.
2. Dip in a mixture of eggs and milk.
3. Fry until golden.

Fun Facts

The Monte Cristo is a variation of the French sandwich Croque-Monsieur.

1 sandwich   480   20

Tuna Melt

A warm and savory sandwich featuring tuna salad and melted cheese.
A classic diner favorite.

Ingredients:

- 2 slices white bread
- 1 can tuna, drained
- 2 tbsp mayonnaise
- 1/4 cup diced celery
- 1/4 cup diced onion
- 2 slices cheddar cheese

Directions

1. Mix tuna, mayonnaise, celery, and onion.
2. Spread tuna salad on bread slices.
3. Top with cheese.
4. Grill until cheese melts.

Fun Facts

Tuna melts were first introduced to American diners in the 1960s.

1 sandwich   600   20

The Classic Club

A triple-decker sensation with ham, turkey, bacon, lettuce, tomato, and mayo. A diner classic.

Ingredients:

- 3 slices toasted white bread
- 2 oz ham
- 2 oz turkey
- 2 strips crispy bacon
- Lettuce and tomato
- Mayonnaise

Directions

1. Layer ham, turkey, bacon, lettuce, tomato, and mayo between bread slices.
2. Secure with toothpicks.

Fun Facts

The Classic Club sandwich has been a staple on diner menus for decades.

1 sandwich 580 30

French Dip with Au Jus

A savory roast beef sandwich served with a side of flavorful au jus for dipping. A French-inspired favorite.

Ingredients:

- 1 French baguette
- 8 oz roast beef
- 2 slices Swiss cheese
- 2 cups beef broth
- 1 tsp Worcestershire sauce
- Salt and pepper to taste

Directions

1. Slice the baguette and add roast beef and Swiss cheese.
2. In a separate pan, heat beef broth and Worcestershire sauce.
3. Season with salt and pepper.
4. Serve for dipping.

Fun Facts

The French Dip sandwich originated in Los Angeles in the early 20th century.

1 sandwich   750   40

Meatball Sub

A hearty sandwich featuring meatballs smothered in marinara sauce and topped with melted cheese.
A taste of Italy.

Ingredients:

- 1 sub roll
- 4 meatballs
- 1/2 cup marinara sauce
- 1/4 cup shredded mozzarella cheese
- 2 tbsp grated Parmesan cheese

Directions

1. Place meatballs in the sub roll.
2. Pour marinara sauce over meatballs.
3. Top with mozzarella and Parmesan.
4. Bake until cheese is bubbly.

Fun Facts

Meatball subs are a popular street food in Italy, especially in Naples.

1 sandwich | 600 | 20

B.L.A.S.T. (Bacon, Lettuce, Avocado, Swiss, Tomato)

A loaded sandwich with crispy bacon, fresh lettuce, creamy avocado, Swiss cheese, and ripe tomatoes.
A flavor explosion.

Ingredients:

- 2 slices whole wheat bread
- 4 strips crispy bacon
- Lettuce, avocado, Swiss cheese, and tomato slices

Directions

1. Layer bacon, lettuce, avocado, Swiss cheese, and tomato between bread slices.
2. Assemble into a sandwich.

Fun Facts

The B.L.A.S.T. sandwich is a modern twist on the classic BLT with added richness from avocado and cheese.

Chapter 4:
Perfect Pastas

2 servings   600   30

Spaghetti and Meatballs

A classic Italian dish with tender meatballs and perfectly cooked spaghetti.
A symbol of comfort and tradition.

Ingredients:

- 8 oz spaghetti
- 1 cup marinara sauce
- 1/2 lb ground beef
- 1/4 cup breadcrumbs
- 1/4 cup grated Parmesan cheese
- 1 egg
- Salt and pepper to taste

Directions

1. Cook spaghetti until al dente.
2. Mix beef, breadcrumbs, Parmesan, egg, salt, and pepper.
3. Form meatballs and bake.
4. Heat marinara sauce and add meatballs.
5. Serve over spaghetti.

Fun Facts

Spaghetti and meatballs is an Italian-American creation, not commonly found in Italy.

4 servings | 500 | 25

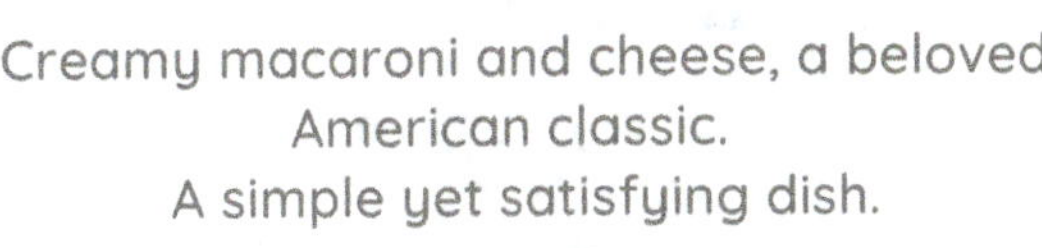

Mac and Cheese

Creamy macaroni and cheese, a beloved American classic.
A simple yet satisfying dish.

Ingredients:

- 8 oz elbow macaroni
- 2 cups shredded cheddar cheese
- 1/2 cup milk
- 2 tbsp butter
- 2 tbsp all-purpose flour
- Salt and pepper to taste

Directions

1. Cook macaroni until tender.
2. In a saucepan, melt butter and whisk in flour.
3. Add milk, cheese, salt, and pepper.
4. Stir until cheese melts.
5. Mix with macaroni.

Fun Facts

Mac and cheese originated in the United States in the 1800s and became popular during the Great Depression.

2 servings | 700 | 20

Fettuccine Alfredo

Silky fettuccine pasta coated in a rich and creamy Alfredo sauce.
A luxurious Italian classic.

Ingredients:

- 8 oz fettuccine pasta
- 1/2 cup heavy cream
- 1/4 cup butter
- 1 cup grated Parmesan cheese
- Salt and white pepper to taste
- Fresh parsley for garnish

Directions

1. Cook fettuccine until al dente.
2. In a pan, heat butter and cream.
3. Stir in Parmesan, salt, and pepper.
4. Toss pasta in the sauce.
5. Garnish with parsley.

Fun Facts

Fettuccine Alfredo was created by Alfredo di Lelio in Rome, Italy, in the early 20th century.

4 servings   650   35

Beef Stroganoff

Normal

Tender strips of beef in a creamy mushroom
sauce served over egg noodles.
A Russian classic.

Ingredients:

- 8 oz egg noodles
- 1 lb beef sirloin, sliced
- 1 cup sliced mushrooms
- 1/2 cup sour cream
- 2 tbsp flour
- 2 tbsp butter
- 1/2 cup beef broth
- 1 onion, chopped

Directions

1. Cook egg noodles.
2. In a skillet, brown beef in butter.
3. Add onions and mushrooms, cook.
4. Stir in flour.
5. Add beef broth and sour cream.
6. Serve over noodles.

Fun Facts

Beef Stroganoff was named after a Russian
noble family and gained popularity in the mid-
19th century.

2 servings   800   40

Chicken Parmesan

Crispy breaded chicken cutlets topped with
marinara sauce and melted cheese.
A comforting Italian-American favorite.

Ingredients:

- 2 chicken breasts
- 1 cup breadcrumbs
- 1 cup marinara sauce
- 1 cup shredded mozzarella cheese
- 1/4 cup grated Parmesan cheese
- 1 egg
- Salt and pepper to taste

Directions

1. Bread chicken with breadcrumbs, egg, salt, and pepper.
2. Bake until crispy.
3. Top with marinara, mozzarella, and Parmesan.
4. Bake until cheese melts.

Fun Facts

Chicken Parmesan, or Chicken Parmigiana, was
inspired by Italian "Melanzane alla Parmigiana"
or Eggplant Parmesan.

6 servings | 800 | 45

Layers of pasta, meat sauce, ricotta, and mozzarella, baked to perfection.
A family-favorite Italian dish.

Classic Lasagna

Ingredients:

- 9 lasagna noodles
- 1 lb ground beef
- 1 cup ricotta cheese
- 2 cups shredded mozzarella cheese
- 2 cups marinara sauce
- 1/4 cup grated Parmesan cheese
- Salt and pepper to taste

Directions

1. Cook lasagna noodles.
2. Brown beef and season.
3. Layer noodles, beef, ricotta, mozzarella, and marinara.
4. Repeat layers.
5. Bake until bubbly.
6. Top with Parmesan.

Fun Facts

Lasagna is one of the oldest pasta dishes, with origins dating back to Ancient Greece.

2 servings 550 30

Succulent shrimp in a garlic, butter, and white wine sauce served over linguine. A seafood lover's delight.

Shrimp Scampi Linguine

Ingredients:

- 8 oz linguine
- 1/2 lb shrimp, peeled and deveined
- 4 cloves garlic, minced
- 2 tbsp butter
- 1/4 cup white wine
- Fresh parsley for garnish

Directions

1. Cook linguine until al dente.
2. Sauté garlic in butter.
3. Add shrimp, cook.
4. Pour in white wine, simmer.
5. Serve over linguine with parsley.

Fun Facts

Shrimp Scampi is an Italian-American dish with strong Italian and Mediterranean influences.

4 servings   700   35

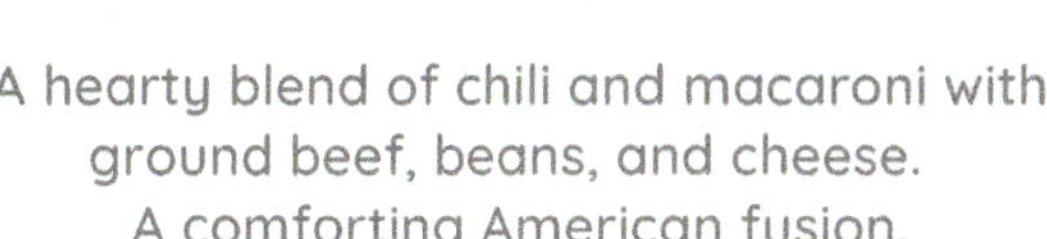

Meaty Chili Mac

A hearty blend of chili and macaroni with ground beef, beans, and cheese.
A comforting American fusion.

Ingredients:

- 8 oz elbow macaroni
- 1/2 lb ground beef
- 1 can chili
- 1 cup shredded cheddar cheese
- 1/2 cup diced onions
- Salt and pepper to taste

Directions

1. Cook macaroni until tender.
2. Brown beef with onions, salt, and pepper.
3. Add chili, cook.
4. Mix with macaroni and top with cheese.
5. Bake until cheese melts.

Fun Facts

Chili Mac is a popular comfort food that combines the flavors of chili and mac and cheese.

2 servings   450   25

Vegetable Primavera

A colorful medley of seasonal vegetables served over pasta with a light cream sauce. A fresh and healthy option.

Ingredients:

- 8 oz fettuccine pasta
- 2 cups mixed vegetables (e.g., bell peppers, broccoli, cherry tomatoes)
- 1/2 cup heavy cream
- 2 tbsp butter
- 1/4 cup grated Parmesan cheese
- Salt and pepper to taste
- Fresh basil for garnish

Directions

1. Cook fettuccine until al dente.
2. Sauté vegetables in butter.
3. Add cream, Parmesan, salt, and pepper.
4. Toss with pasta.
5. Garnish with basil.

Fun Facts

Pasta Primavera was invented in the 1970s by a New York chef, Sirio Maccioni.

4 servings | 650 | 30

Baked Ziti

Ziti pasta baked with marinara sauce, ricotta, mozzarella, and Parmesan.
A satisfying Italian-American classic.

Ingredients:

- 8 oz ziti pasta
- 2 cups marinara sauce
- 1 cup ricotta cheese
- 2 cups shredded mozzarella cheese
- 1/4 cup grated Parmesan cheese
- Fresh basil for garnish

Directions

1. Cook ziti until al dente.
2. Mix ziti with marinara, ricotta, mozzarella, and Parmesan.
3. Bake until bubbly.
4. Garnish with basil.

Fun Facts

Baked ziti is a popular Italian-American dish, often served at family gatherings and potlucks.

Chapter 5:
Homestyle Sides

4 servings | 300 | 30

Mashed Potatoes with Gravy

Creamy mashed potatoes smothered in rich, savory gravy.
A comforting side dish for any meal.

Ingredients:

- 4 large potatoes, peeled and diced
- 1/2 cup milk
- 4 tbsp butter
- Salt and pepper to taste
- 1 cup beef or chicken gravy

Directions

1. Boil potatoes until tender.
2. Mash with milk, butter, salt, and pepper.
3. Heat gravy and serve over potatoes.

Fun Facts

Mashed potatoes were a favorite of Thomas Jefferson, who introduced them to the United States in the late 18th century.

4 servings   400   25

Crispy Onion Rings

Golden, crispy onion rings, the perfect side for burgers and sandwiches.
A classic American favorite.

Ingredients:

- 2 large onions, cut into rings
- 1 cup all-purpose flour
- 1 cup buttermilk
- 1 cup breadcrumbs
- Salt and pepper to taste
- Oil for frying

Directions

1. Dip onion rings in flour.
2. Dip in buttermilk.
3. Coat with breadcrumbs, salt, and pepper.
4. Fry until golden brown.

Fun Facts

Onion rings date back to the early 20th century and were popularized in the United States.

2 servings | 450 | 40

Loaded Baked Potato

A baked potato loaded with sour cream, cheddar cheese, bacon, and chives. A side dish with indulgence.

Ingredients:

- 2 large russet potatoes
- 1/2 cup sour cream
- 1/2 cup shredded cheddar cheese
- 4 strips crispy bacon, crumbled
- Chopped chives
- Salt and pepper to taste

Directions

1. Bake potatoes until tender.
2. Slice and fluff the insides.
3. Top with sour cream, cheese, bacon, chives, salt, and pepper.

Fun Facts

The loaded baked potato became popular in restaurants in the mid-20th century as a side or appetizer.

4 servings   200   15

Homestyle Coleslaw

A refreshing coleslaw made with cabbage, carrots, and a creamy dressing.
A classic barbecue side.

Ingredients:

- 4 cups shredded cabbage
- 1/2 cup shredded carrots
- 1/2 cup mayonnaise
- 2 tbsp white vinegar
- 2 tbsp sugar
- Salt and pepper to taste

Directions

1. In a bowl, combine cabbage and carrots.
2. In a separate bowl, mix mayonnaise, vinegar, sugar, salt, and pepper.
3. Toss dressing with cabbage and carrots.

Fun Facts

Coleslaw has been enjoyed for centuries and is believed to have originated in Ancient Rome.

4 servings | 350 | 35

Crispy Tater Tots

Golden and crispy tater tots, a favorite side dish for kids and adults alike.
A convenient snack.

Ingredients:

- 2 cups frozen tater tots
- Salt and pepper to taste

Directions

1. Preheat the oven and bake tater tots according to the package instructions.
2. Season with salt and pepper.
3. Serve hot.

Fun Facts

Tater tots were created in the 1950s by two American brothers and quickly became popular in schools.

6 biscuits   300   30

Biscuits with Honey Butter

Flaky and tender biscuits served with sweet and creamy honey butter.
A Southern comfort classic.

Ingredients:

- 2 cups all-purpose flour
- 2 tbsp sugar
- 2 1/2 tsp baking powder
- 1/2 cup cold butter
- 1/2 cup buttermilk
- Salt to taste
- 1/2 cup butter
- 1/4 cup honey

Directions

1. Preheat the oven.
2. Mix flour, sugar, baking powder, and salt.
3. Cut in cold butter.
4. Stir in buttermilk.
5. Form biscuits and bake.
6. Mix butter and honey for the topping.

Fun Facts

Biscuits have a long history, with origins dating back to ancient Egypt.

4 servings   450   25

Seasoned Curly Fries

Curly, crispy fries seasoned with a blend of savory spices.
A fun and flavorful side.

Ingredients:

- 2 cups frozen curly fries
- 1 tbsp vegetable oil
- 1 tsp paprika
- 1/2 tsp garlic powder
- 1/2 tsp onion powder
- Salt and pepper to taste

Directions

1. Preheat the oven and bake curly fries according to the package instructions.
2. Toss with a mixture of oil, paprika, garlic powder, onion powder, salt, and pepper.
3. Serve hot.

Fun Facts

Curly fries were first introduced to the fast food scene in the 1970s.

4 servings | 250 | 20

Creamed Spinach

A velvety side dish featuring tender spinach in
a rich and creamy sauce.
A classic steakhouse side.

Ingredients:

- 8 cups fresh spinach
- 1/2 cup heavy cream
- 2 tbsp butter
- 2 cloves garlic, minced
- 1/4 cup grated Parmesan cheese
- Salt and pepper to taste

Directions

1. Sauté garlic in butter.
2. Add spinach and cook until wilted.
3. Stir in cream, Parmesan, salt, and pepper.
4. Cook until thickened.

Fun Facts

Creamed spinach has been a popular side dish
for steaks and roasts since the 19th century.

4 servings | 300 | 30

Fried Pickles

Crispy and tangy pickles coated in a seasoned batter and fried to perfection.
A unique and delicious side.

Ingredients:

- 2 cups dill pickle slices
- 1 cup buttermilk
- 1 cup all-purpose flour
- 1 tsp paprika
- 1/2 tsp garlic powder
- Salt and pepper to taste
- Oil for frying

Directions

1. Soak pickle slices in buttermilk.
2. Mix flour, paprika, garlic powder, salt, and pepper.
3. Coat pickles in the flour mixture.
4. Fry until golden.

Fun Facts

Fried pickles are believed to have originated in the southern United States.

4 servings | 400 | 30

Sweet Potato Fries

Crispy and slightly sweet sweet potato fries, a healthier alternative to regular fries.
A modern classic.

Ingredients:

- 2 large sweet potatoes, cut into fries
- 2 tbsp olive oil
- 1 tsp paprika
- 1/2 tsp cinnamon
- Salt and pepper to taste

Directions

1. Preheat the oven and toss sweet potato fries with olive oil, paprika, cinnamon, salt, and pepper.
2. Bake until crispy.

Fun Facts

Sweet potato fries gained popularity in the late 20th century as a nutritious and tasty side dish.

Chapter 6:
Soups and Salads

4 servings   300   45

Chicken Noodle Soup

Normal

A comforting and nourishing soup with tender chicken, vegetables, and noodles.
A timeless classic.

Ingredients:

- 2 boneless, skinless chicken breasts
- 8 cups chicken broth
- 2 carrots, sliced
- 2 celery stalks, chopped
- 1 cup egg noodles
- 1 onion, chopped
- 2 cloves garlic, minced
- Salt and pepper to taste

Directions

1. Boil chicken breasts in broth until cooked.
2. Remove and shred chicken.
3. Add vegetables, noodles, chicken, and garlic to the broth.
4. Simmer until noodles are tender.
5. Season with salt and pepper.

Fun Facts

Chicken noodle soup is believed to have originated from Jewish cuisine and was popularized in the United States.

4 servings 250 20

Classic Caesar Salad

A crisp romaine lettuce salad with garlic croutons, Parmesan cheese, and Caesar dressing.
A favorite in fine dining.

Ingredients:

- 1 head romaine lettuce, torn
- 1 cup croutons
- 1/2 cup grated Parmesan cheese
- Caesar dressing (store-bought or homemade)

Directions

1. Toss lettuce with croutons and Parmesan.
2. Drizzle with Caesar dressing.
3. Mix until well-coated.

Fun Facts

The Caesar salad was created by Caesar Cardini, an Italian-American chef, in Tijuana, Mexico, in the 1920s.

4 servings   400   30

Tomato Soup with Grilled Cheese

Creamy tomato soup paired with a gooey
grilled cheese sandwich.
A classic comfort food duo.

Ingredients:

- 2 cups tomato soup (canned or homemade)
- 4 slices white bread
- 4 slices cheddar cheese
- Butter for grilling

Directions

1. Heat tomato soup in a pot.
2. Butter one side of each bread slice.
3. Place cheese between slices (butter side out).
4. Grill until golden.
5. Serve with tomato soup.

Fun Facts

Tomato soup and grilled cheese sandwiches have been a popular pairing in the United States since the mid-20th century.

4 servings   550   20

Cobb Salad

A hearty salad featuring chopped chicken, bacon, eggs, avocado, and blue cheese. A satisfying meal in a bowl.

Ingredients:

- 2 cups cooked chicken breast, diced
- 1/2 cup crumbled blue cheese
- 4 cups mixed salad greens
- 2 hard-boiled eggs, sliced
- 4 strips crispy bacon, crumbled
- 1 avocado, diced
- 1/2 cup vinaigrette dressing

Directions

1. Arrange salad greens in a bowl.
2. Top with chicken, blue cheese, eggs, bacon, and avocado.
3. Drizzle with vinaigrette.

Fun Facts

The Cobb salad was created at the Hollywood Brown Derby restaurant in the 1930s.

4 servings   400   40

New England Clam Chowder

A creamy and rich soup made with tender clams, potatoes, and bacon.
A taste of the East Coast.

Ingredients:

- 2 cups chopped clams
- 2 cups diced potatoes
- 1/2 cup diced onion
- 4 strips crispy bacon, crumbled
- 2 cups whole milk
- 2 cups chicken broth
- 2 tbsp butter
- Salt and pepper to taste

Directions

1. In a pot, sauté onions in butter.
2. Add potatoes, milk, and chicken broth.
3. Simmer until potatoes are tender.
4. Stir in clams and bacon.
5. Season with salt and pepper.

Fun Facts

Clam chowder is a classic dish of New England, particularly popular in Massachusetts and Maine.

4 servings — 300 kcal — 15

Greek Salad

A refreshing salad with cucumbers, tomatoes, olives, feta cheese, and a zesty vinaigrette. A taste of the Mediterranean.

Ingredients:

- 2 cups diced cucumbers
- 2 cups diced tomatoes
- 1/2 cup sliced Kalamata olives
- 1/2 cup crumbled feta cheese
- Red onion slices
- 1/4 cup extra-virgin olive oil
- 2 tbsp red wine vinegar
- Fresh oregano for garnish
- Salt and pepper to taste

Directions

1. Combine cucumbers, tomatoes, olives, and feta.
2. Drizzle with olive oil and vinegar.
3. Garnish with oregano, salt, and pepper.

Fun Facts

Greek salad, or Horiatiki, is a traditional dish of Greek cuisine with ancient origins.

4 servings | 350 | 60

Split Pea Soup

A hearty and flavorful soup made from dried
split peas, ham, and vegetables.
A satisfying and nutritious option.

Ingredients:

- 2 cups split green peas
- 1 cup diced ham
- 1/2 cup diced carrots
- 1/2 cup diced onion
- 2 cloves garlic, minced
- 8 cups water or chicken broth
- 1 bay leaf
- Salt and pepper to taste

Directions

1. Rinse split peas.
2. Combine peas, ham, carrots, onion, garlic, water or broth, and bay leaf in a pot.
3. Simmer until peas are tender.
4. Remove bay leaf.
5. Season with salt and pepper.

Fun Facts

Split pea soup has been enjoyed for centuries
and is particularly popular in Northern Europe
and North America.

4 servings   350   20

Chef's Salad

A versatile salad with mixed greens, assorted cold cuts, cheese, and a vinaigrette dressing. A customizable delight.

Ingredients:

- 4 cups mixed salad greens
- 1/2 cup diced ham
- 1/2 cup diced turkey or chicken
- 1/2 cup sliced Swiss cheese
- 1/2 cup cheddar cheese
- 1/2 cup grape tomatoes
- Hard-boiled eggs, sliced
- 1/4 cup vinaigrette dressing

Directions

1. Arrange salad greens on a plate.
2. Top with ham, turkey or chicken, Swiss cheese, cheddar cheese, grape tomatoes, and eggs.
3. Drizzle with vinaigrette.

Fun Facts

Chef's salad offers endless variations based on your favorite cold cuts and cheeses.

6 servings   450   60

Chili

A hearty and spicy stew made with ground beef, beans, tomatoes, and a blend of chili spices.
A favorite for chili lovers.

Ingredients:

- 1 lb ground beef
- 1 onion, chopped
- 2 cloves garlic, minced
- 1 can kidney beans
- 1 can black beans
- 1 can diced tomatoes
- 2 cups beef broth
- 2 tbsp chili powder
- 1 tsp cumin
- Salt and pepper to taste

Directions

1. In a pot, brown beef with onions and garlic.
2. Add beans, tomatoes, beef broth, and spices.
3. Simmer until flavors meld.
4. Season with salt and pepper.

Fun Facts

Chili is a beloved dish with a long history, often enjoyed during chilly weather and at cook-offs.

4 servings | 350 | 15

Wedge Salad with Blue Cheese Dressing

A classic wedge of iceberg lettuce drizzled with creamy blue cheese dressing and garnished with bacon and chives.
A timeless favorite.

Ingredients:

- 1 head iceberg lettuce, cut into wedges
- 1/2 cup blue cheese dressing (store-bought or homemade)
- 4 strips crispy bacon, crumbled
- Chopped chives
- Salt and pepper to taste

Directions

1. Place lettuce wedges on plates.
2. Drizzle with blue cheese dressing.
3. Sprinkle with bacon, chives, salt, and pepper.

Fun Facts

The wedge salad has been a staple of classic American steakhouse menus for decades.

We have a small favor to ask

As we journey through the heart of American nostalgia in the "Best of Diner Classics Cookbook: A Taste of Nostalgia - 100+ Best Copycat Classic American Dinners Recipes," I want to pause for a moment to share something important.

Reviews, my fellow seekers of comfort in culinary classics, are like the familiar booths in a diner—essential, warm, and inviting. For a small publisher like us, they are the neon signs that illuminate our culinary journey.

If you can spare a moment, I implore you to revisit the platform where you discovered this homage to diner delights—whether it's an app or an online marketplace. There, like the jukebox in the corner, you'll find the review button. We would be immensely grateful if you could grace us with your honest rating and a brief, flavorful sentence capturing your diner experience.

Every review is a sip of coffee for us. They're the conversations overheard in the bustling diner, adding character and depth to our culinary narrative. In the spirit of honesty, should you encounter a minor hiccup within these pages, please know we've meticulously crafted this diner journey. We're not infallible, and, much like a diner missing a beloved dish, small mistakes can happen. We hope you can savor the overall experience despite these minor imperfections.

Your support, conveyed through a review, is like the perfect bite of a diner burger—it completes the experience and fuels our passion to keep serving up classic American dinners. So, please, take a moment, and let your words be the extra dash of nostalgia in our diner classics.

We deeply appreciate your time, your discerning palate, and your love for the timeless art of diner cuisine. After all, this cookbook isn't just about recipes; it's about celebrating the cherished flavors of classic American diners with fellow aficionados. With sincere gratitude and a virtual booth reserved for you, we eagerly await your feedback. Now, let's return to the recipes and continue this culinary journey together.

Chapter 7:
Diner Dessert Classics

8 servings   350   60

Old-Fashioned Apple Pie

A comforting and timeless dessert with sweet, spiced apples in a flaky crust.
A slice of nostalgia.

Ingredients:

- 6 cups sliced apples (e.g., Granny Smith or Golden Delicious)
- 1 cup granulated sugar
- 1 tsp cinnamon
- 1/4 tsp nutmeg
- 2 pie crusts (homemade or store-bought)
- 2 tbsp butter

Directions

1. Preheat the oven.
2. Toss apples with sugar, cinnamon, and nutmeg.
3. Line a pie dish with one crust.
4. Add apples and dot with butter.
5. Cover with the second crust.
6. Bake until golden brown.

Fun Facts

Apple pie is an American classic with a history dating back to the early 17th century.

4 servings — 500 — 40

Chocolate Fudge Brownie Sundae

Decadent chocolate fudge brownies topped with ice cream, hot fudge, and whipped cream. A chocolate lover's dream.

Ingredients:

- 4 chocolate fudge brownies
- 4 scoops of your favorite ice cream
- 1/2 cup hot fudge sauce
- Whipped cream
- Maraschino cherries

Directions

1. Warm the brownies.
2. Place each brownie on a serving plate.
3. Top with a scoop of ice cream.
4. Drizzle with hot fudge.
5. Garnish with whipped cream and a cherry.

Fun Facts

The brownie sundae is a beloved dessert that gained popularity in the United States in the 20th century.

2 servings   400   15

Banana Split

A classic dessert featuring banana halves, ice cream, chocolate, and fruit toppings. A sweet and fruity delight.

Ingredients:

- 2 ripe bananas, split lengthwise
- 4 scoops of ice cream (vanilla, chocolate, and strawberry)
- Chocolate syrup
- Strawberry topping
- Pineapple topping
- Whipped cream
- Chopped nuts
- Maraschino cherries

Directions

1. Place banana halves in a serving dish.
2. Top with scoops of ice cream.
3. Drizzle with chocolate, strawberry, and pineapple toppings.
4. Garnish with whipped cream, nuts, and cherries.

Fun Facts

The banana split was created in the early 20th century and became an iconic ice cream parlor dessert.

8 servings   450   60

Classic Cheesecake

A velvety and rich cheesecake with a graham cracker crust.
A timeless dessert for any occasion.

Ingredients:

- 2 cups graham cracker crumbs
- 1/2 cup melted butter
- 4 (8 oz) packages cream cheese, softened
- 1 1/2 cups granulated sugar
- 1 tsp vanilla extract
- 4 large eggs
- 1 cup sour cream
- 1/4 cup all-purpose flour

Directions

1. Preheat the oven.
2. Mix graham cracker crumbs and melted butter, then press into the base of a springform pan.
3. In a bowl, beat cream cheese, sugar, and vanilla until smooth.
4. Add eggs one at a time, then stir in sour cream and flour.
5. Pour over crust.
6. Bake until set.

Fun Facts

Cheesecake has ancient Greek roots and evolved into the dessert we know today in the United States.

4 servings   350   30

Strawberry Shortcake

Easy

Sweet, juicy strawberries served over a fluffy biscuit with whipped cream. A delightful summer treat.

Ingredients:

- 2 cups fresh strawberries, sliced
- 1/4 cup granulated sugar
- 4 baked biscuits (homemade or store-bought)
- Whipped cream

Directions

1. Toss strawberries with sugar and let sit.
2. Split biscuits in half.
3. Top with strawberries and whipped cream.

Fun Facts

Strawberry shortcake has been enjoyed in the United States since the 19th century, particularly in the summer.

8 servings | 400 | 60

Lemon Meringue Pie

A tangy and sweet lemon filling topped with a
fluffy meringue in a buttery pie crust.
A zesty classic.

Ingredients:

- 1 (9-inch) pie crust (homemade or store-bought)
- 1 cup granulated sugar
- 2 tbsp all-purpose flour
- 2 tbsp cornstarch
- 1 1/2 cups water
- 4 large egg yolks
- Zest and juice of 2 lemons
- 2 tbsp butter
- 4 large egg whites
- 1/4 cup granulated sugar

Fun Facts

Lemon meringue pie is a classic American
dessert with a bright and zesty flavor.

Directions

1. Preheat the oven.
2. Bake the pie crust and let it cool.
3. In a saucepan, mix sugar, flour, and cornstarch.
4. Gradually stir in water, egg yolks, lemon zest, and juice.
5. Cook until thick.
6. Remove from heat, stir in butter, and pour into the crust.
7. Beat egg whites until stiff, gradually adding sugar.
8. Spread meringue over the filling, sealing the edges.
9. Bake until golden brown.

12 servings | 450 | 60

Red Velvet Cake

A moist and velvety red cake with cream cheese frosting.
A southern classic with a touch of luxury.

Ingredients:

- 2 1/2 cups all-purpose flour
- 1 1/2 cups granulated sugar
- 1 tsp baking powder
- 1 tsp baking soda
- 1 tsp cocoa powder
- 1 1/2 cups vegetable oil
- 1 cup buttermilk
- 2 large eggs
- Red food coloring
- 1 tsp vanilla extract
- 1 tsp white vinegar
- 1 (8 oz) package cream cheese
- 1/2 cup butter
- 4 cups powdered sugar
- 1 tsp vanilla extract

Directions

1. Preheat the oven.
2. In a bowl, sift together flour, sugar, baking powder, baking soda, and cocoa.
3. In another bowl, mix oil, buttermilk, eggs, food coloring, vanilla, and vinegar.
4. Add dry ingredients and mix until smooth.
5. Pour into cake pans and bake.
6. Beat cream cheese, butter, powdered sugar, and vanilla for frosting.
7. Frost the cooled cake.

Fun Facts

Red velvet cake is believed to have originated in the southern United States in the 19th century.

6 servings | 400 | 45

Bread Pudding with Whiskey Sauce

A warm and comforting dessert made from stale bread, raisins, and a rich whiskey sauce. A taste of home.

Ingredients:

- 4 cups cubed stale bread
- 1/2 cup raisins
- 4 cups milk
- 1 cup granulated sugar
- 2 large eggs
- 2 tbsp butter
- 1 tsp vanilla extract
- 1/4 tsp cinnamon
- 1/4 cup whiskey

Directions

1. Preheat the oven.
2. Combine bread and raisins in a baking dish.
3. In a saucepan, heat milk but do not boil.
4. In a bowl, whisk sugar, eggs, butter, vanilla, and cinnamon.
5. Gradually add hot milk.
6. Pour over bread and raisins.
7. Bake until set.
8. In a small saucepan, heat whiskey, sugar, and butter for the sauce.
9. Serve sauce over bread pudding.

Fun Facts

Bread pudding is a thrifty and delicious dessert that has been enjoyed for generations.

2 servings | 250 | 5

Root Beer Float

A simple and delightful dessert drink made
with root beer and vanilla ice cream.
A fizzy and fun treat.

Ingredients:

- 2 scoops of vanilla ice cream
- 1 can of root beer

Directions

1. Place ice cream scoops in a glass.
2. Pour root beer over the ice cream.
3. Serve with a straw and a long spoon.

Fun Facts

The root beer float is a classic soda fountain
creation that dates back to the late 19th century.

8 servings | 350 | 60

Blueberry Pie

A sweet and juicy blueberry filling in a flaky pie crust.
A delightful summer dessert.

Ingredients:

- 2 cups fresh or frozen blueberries
- 1 cup granulated sugar
- 1/4 cup cornstarch
- 1/4 tsp salt
- 1/2 tsp cinnamon
- 1/4 tsp almond extract
- 1 (9-inch) pie crust (homemade or store-bought)
- 1 tbsp butter

Directions

1. Preheat the oven.
2. Mix blueberries, sugar, cornstarch, salt, cinnamon, and almond extract.
3. Pour into pie crust.
4. Dot with butter.
5. Cover with a second crust or lattice top.
6. Bake until filling is bubbling and crust is golden brown.

Fun Facts

Blueberry pie is a classic American dessert, especially popular in regions where blueberries are abundant.

Chapter 8:
Comforting Casseroles

6 servings   400   60

Chicken Pot Pie

A warm and savory casserole filled with tender chicken, vegetables, and a flaky pastry crust. A true comfort classic.

Ingredients:

- 2 cups cooked chicken, diced
- 2 cups frozen mixed vegetables
- 1/3 cup butter
- 1/3 cup chopped onion
- 1/3 cup all-purpose flour
- 1/2 tsp salt
- 1/4 tsp black pepper
- 1 3/4 cups chicken broth
- 2/3 cup milk
- 2 (9-inch) pie crusts (homemade or store-bought)

Directions

1. Preheat the oven.
2. In a saucepan, melt butter and sauté onions.
3. Stir in flour, salt, and pepper.
4. Gradually add broth and milk.
5. Cook until thick.
6. Mix in chicken and vegetables.
7. Pour into one pie crust.
8. Cover with the second crust.
9. Bake until golden brown.

Fun Facts

Chicken pot pie has been a beloved American comfort food for generations.

6 servings   450   40

Tater Tot Casserole

A hearty and indulgent casserole made with tater tots, ground beef, cheese, and a creamy sauce.
A kid-friendly favorite.

Ingredients:

- 1 lb ground beef
- 1/2 cup chopped onion
- 1 can cream of mushroom soup
- 1 cup sour cream
- 2 cups shredded cheddar cheese
- 1 (32 oz) package frozen tater tots

Directions

1. Preheat the oven.
2. In a skillet, brown ground beef with onions.
3. Stir in soup, sour cream, and half the cheese.
4. Spread mixture in a baking dish.
5. Arrange tater tots on top.
6. Bake until tater tots are crispy.
7. Sprinkle with remaining cheese.

Fun Facts

Tater tot casserole, often known as "hotdish," is a Midwestern comfort food tradition in the United States.

6 servings | 400 | 60

Beef and Vegetable Shepherd's Pie

A hearty and savory casserole with ground beef, vegetables, and creamy mashed potatoes.
A taste of the British Isles.

Ingredients:

- 1 lb ground beef
- 1 cup chopped onion
- 1 cup frozen peas and carrots
- 1/2 cup frozen corn
- 1 can tomato soup
- 2 cups mashed potatoes (prepared)
- 1/2 cup shredded cheddar cheese

Directions

1. Preheat the oven.
2. In a skillet, brown ground beef with onions.
3. Add vegetables and tomato soup.
4. Pour mixture into a baking dish.
5. Top with mashed potatoes and cheese.
6. Bake until bubbly and golden.

Fun Facts

Shepherd's pie is a traditional British dish that originated as a frugal way to use leftover roast meat.

6 servings   350   40

Broccoli and Cheese Casserole

A creamy and cheesy casserole with tender broccoli florets.
A classic side dish with comfort appeal.

Ingredients:

- 4 cups fresh broccoli florets
- 1 cup shredded cheddar cheese
- 1 cup mayonnaise
- 1 cup sour cream
- 1/2 cup grated Parmesan cheese
- 2 large eggs, beaten
- 1 cup breadcrumbs
- 2 tbsp butter, melted

Directions

1. Preheat the oven.
2. Steam broccoli until tender.
3. In a bowl, combine cheddar cheese, mayonnaise, sour cream, Parmesan cheese, and eggs.
4. Place broccoli in a baking dish and spread the cheese mixture on top.
5. Combine breadcrumbs and melted butter, then sprinkle on the casserole.
6. Bake until golden and bubbly.

Fun Facts

Broccoli and cheese casserole has been a popular side dish in American cuisine for decades.

6 servings   400   60

Chicken and Rice Casserole

A satisfying casserole with tender chicken, rice, and a creamy sauce.
A family favorite.

Ingredients:

- 2 cups cooked chicken, diced
- 1 cup white rice, cooked
- 1 cup sour cream
- 1 cup mayonnaise
- 1 can cream of chicken soup
- 1 cup grated cheddar cheese
- 1/2 cup sliced almonds
- 1/2 cup chopped onion

Directions

1. Preheat the oven.
2. In a large bowl, combine chicken, rice, sour cream, mayonnaise, cream of chicken soup, and half the cheese.
3. Pour mixture into a baking dish.
4. Sprinkle with remaining cheese, almonds, and onions.
5. Bake until bubbly and golden.

Fun Facts

Chicken and rice casserole is a comforting dish often served at family gatherings and potlucks.

6 servings | 350 | 60

Stuffed Bell Pepper Casserole

All the flavors of stuffed bell peppers in an
easy-to-make casserole.
A comforting meal with a twist.

Ingredients:

- 1 lb ground beef
- 4 large bell peppers, chopped
- 1 cup chopped onion
- 1 can diced tomatoes
- 1 cup cooked rice
- 1 cup tomato sauce
- 1 cup shredded cheddar cheese

Directions

1. Preheat the oven.
2. In a skillet, brown ground beef with peppers and onions.
3. Stir in diced tomatoes and cooked rice.
4. Pour mixture into a baking dish.
5. Drizzle with tomato sauce and sprinkle with cheese.
6. Bake until cheese is melted and bubbly.

Fun Facts

Stuffed bell pepper casserole simplifies the classic stuffed pepper recipe for a fuss-free meal.

6 servings   350   60

Sausage and Egg Breakfast Casserole

A satisfying and hearty breakfast casserole with sausage, eggs, cheese, and bread. A great start to the day.

Ingredients:

- 1 lb breakfast sausage
- 6 slices bread, cubed
- 2 cups shredded cheddar cheese
- 6 large eggs
- 2 cups milk
- 1/2 tsp salt
- 1/4 tsp black pepper
- 1/4 tsp dry mustard

Directions

1. Preheat the oven.
2. Brown sausage in a skillet, then drain.
3. In a baking dish, layer bread cubes, cooked sausage, and cheddar cheese.
4. In a bowl, beat eggs, milk, salt, pepper, and mustard.
5. Pour over the layered ingredients.
6. Cover and refrigerate overnight.
7. Bake until set.

Fun Facts

Breakfast casseroles like this one are a popular choice for brunches and special mornings.

6 servings | 300 | 30

Spinach and Artichoke Dip

A creamy and indulgent dip made with spinach, artichokes, and melted cheese. A crowd-pleaser at parties.

Ingredients:

- 1 (10 oz) package frozen chopped spinach, thawed and drained
- 1 (14 oz) can artichoke hearts, drained and chopped
- 1 cup grated Parmesan cheese
- 1 cup mayonnaise
- 1 cup sour cream
- 1 cup shredded mozzarella cheese
- 1 tsp minced garlic
- 1/2 tsp salt
- 1/2 tsp black pepper

Directions

1. Preheat the oven.
2. In a bowl, mix spinach, artichoke hearts, Parmesan cheese, mayonnaise, sour cream, mozzarella cheese, garlic, salt, and pepper.
3. Transfer to a baking dish.
4. Bake until bubbly and golden.
5. Serve with chips or bread.

Fun Facts

Spinach and artichoke dip is a popular appetizer often found on restaurant menus.

6 servings | 250 | 30

Classic Green Bean Casserole

A simple yet delicious casserole with green beans, creamy mushroom sauce, and crispy fried onions.
A staple at holiday feasts.

Ingredients:

- 2 (14.5 oz) cans green beans, drained
- 1 (10.5 oz) can cream of mushroom soup
- 1/2 cup milk
- 1 1/3 cups French-fried onions

Directions

1. Preheat the oven.
2. Mix green beans, mushroom soup, and milk in a baking dish.
3. Bake until hot.
4. Top with fried onions.
5. Bake until onions are golden.

Fun Facts

Green bean casserole is a beloved side dish, especially during Thanksgiving and other holiday meals.

6 servings   450   45

Mac and Cheese Casserole

A creamy and cheesy casserole with elbow macaroni and a golden breadcrumb topping. A childhood favorite, all grown up.

Ingredients:

- 2 cups elbow macaroni, cooked
- 2 cups shredded cheddar cheese
- 1/2 cup grated Parmesan cheese
- 3 cups milk
- 1/4 cup butter
- 2 1/2 cups breadcrumbs
- 2 tbsp butter, melted
- Salt and pepper to taste

Directions

1. Preheat the oven.
2. Mix cooked macaroni with cheddar and Parmesan cheese.
3. In a saucepan, melt butter, then add flour, milk, salt, and pepper.
4. Cook until thick.
5. Pour sauce over macaroni and cheese.
6. Combine breadcrumbs with melted butter.
7. Sprinkle over the casserole.
8. Bake until bubbly and golden.

Fun Facts

Mac and cheese casserole transforms a classic comfort food into a rich and satisfying dish.

Chapter 9:
Homestyle Meaty Mainstays

6 servings   400   70

A classic American meatloaf with a rich, savory gravy.
A comforting staple.

Meatloaf with Gravy

Ingredients:

- 1 1/2 lbs ground beef
- 1/2 lb ground pork
- 1 cup breadcrumbs
- 1/2 cup chopped onion
- 1/2 cup chopped bell pepper
- 2 cloves garlic, minced
- 2 large eggs
- 1/2 cup ketchup
- 1/4 cup milk
- 1 tsp salt
- 1/2 tsp black pepper
- 1/2 tsp dried thyme
- 1/2 tsp dried rosemary
- 1/2 cup beef broth
- 1/4 cup all-purpose flour

Directions

1. Preheat the oven.
2. In a large bowl, combine beef, pork, breadcrumbs, onion, bell pepper, garlic, eggs, ketchup, milk, salt, pepper, thyme, and rosemary.
3. Shape into a loaf and place in a baking dish.
4. Bake until cooked through.
5. In a saucepan, whisk flour into beef broth.
6. Cook until thick and pour over the meatloaf.

Fun Facts

Meatloaf is a comforting dish with roots dating back to ancient times, but it gained popularity in the United States during the 20th century.

4 servings   450   45

Chicken Fried Chicken

Normal

Tender chicken breasts breaded and fried to perfection.
A southern classic.

Ingredients:

- 4 boneless, skinless chicken breasts
- 2 cups buttermilk
- 2 cups all-purpose flour
- 1 tsp salt
- 1/2 tsp black pepper
- 1/2 tsp paprika
- 1/4 tsp cayenne pepper
- Vegetable oil for frying
- Gravy for serving (optional)

Directions

1. Pound chicken breasts to an even thickness.
2. Soak in buttermilk.
3. In a shallow dish, combine flour, salt, pepper, paprika, and cayenne.
4. Dredge chicken in the flour mixture.
5. Heat oil in a skillet and fry chicken until golden and cooked through.
6. Serve with gravy if desired.

Fun Facts

Chicken fried chicken is a southern comfort food favorite, often served with mashed potatoes and gravy.

4 servings   350   40

Juicy pork chops served with sweet and tangy applesauce.
A perfect balance of flavors.

Pork Chops with Applesauce

Ingredients:

- 4 bone-in pork chops
- Salt and pepper to taste
- 2 tbsp vegetable oil
- 2 apples, peeled, cored, and sliced
- 2 tbsp brown sugar
- 1/2 tsp cinnamon
- 1/2 cup water

Directions

1. Season pork chops with salt and pepper.
2. In a skillet, heat oil and brown pork chops.
3. Remove pork chops and set aside.
4. In the same skillet, sauté apples, brown sugar, and cinnamon until tender.
5. Add water and simmer until apples are soft.
6. Serve pork chops with applesauce.

Fun Facts

Pork chops with applesauce is a classic combination that balances the savory and sweet flavors.

4 servings   300   30

Liver and Onions

Pan-fried liver with tender caramelized onions.
A hearty and old-school dish.

Ingredients:

- 1 lb beef or calf liver, sliced
- Salt and pepper to taste
- 1/2 cup all-purpose flour
- 2 large onions, thinly sliced
- 4 tbsp butter
- 1/2 cup beef broth

Directions

1. Season liver with salt and pepper.
2. Dredge liver in flour.
3. In a skillet, melt butter and cook liver until browned.
4. Remove liver and set aside.
5. In the same skillet, sauté onions until caramelized.
6. Add beef broth and simmer.
7. Serve liver with onions.

Fun Facts

Liver and onions is a traditional dish with a long history, appreciated for its rich flavor.

4 servings | 350 | 40

Beef Liver with Bacon

Slices of beef liver cooked with crispy bacon.
A bold and robust dish.

Ingredients:

- 1 lb beef liver, sliced
- Salt and pepper to taste
- 4 slices bacon
- 1 large onion, thinly sliced
- 1/2 cup all-purpose flour
- 1/2 cup beef broth

Directions

1. Season liver with salt and pepper.
2. Wrap each liver slice with a slice of bacon.
3. Dredge in flour.
4. In a skillet, cook bacon-wrapped liver until bacon is crispy and liver is cooked.
5. Remove and set aside.
6. In the same skillet, sauté onions until tender.
7. Add beef broth and simmer.
8. Serve liver with onions.

Fun Facts

Beef liver with bacon is a dish enjoyed by those who appreciate its strong and distinctive flavor.

6 servings | 400 | 60

Chicken and Dumplings

Tender chicken and fluffy dumplings in a comforting broth.
A southern classic.

Ingredients:

- 4 boneless, skinless chicken breasts
- Salt and pepper to taste
- 2 cups all-purpose flour
- 2 tsp baking powder
- 1/2 tsp salt
- 1 cup milk
- 2 cups chicken broth
- 1/2 cup heavy cream
- 2 tbsp butter
- 2 cups frozen mixed vegetables

Directions

1. Season chicken with salt and pepper and cook until done.
2. In a bowl, mix flour, baking powder, and salt.
3. Add milk and stir until a dough forms.
4. Roll out dough and cut into dumplings.
5. In a pot, combine chicken broth, heavy cream, and butter.
6. Bring to a simmer and add dumplings.
7. Simmer until dumplings are cooked.
8. Add cooked chicken and vegetables.
9. Simmer until heated through.

Fun Facts

Chicken and dumplings is a beloved southern dish that combines hearty dumplings with tender chicken in a flavorful broth.

6 servings | 350 | 60

Beef and Mushroom Pot Roast

A tender pot roast with mushrooms and a rich gravy.
A hearty and satisfying meal.

Ingredients:

- 3 lbs beef chuck roast
- Salt and pepper to taste
- 2 tbsp vegetable oil
- 1 onion, sliced
- 2 cups sliced mushrooms
- 2 cloves garlic, minced
- 2 cups beef broth
- 1/2 cup red wine (optional)
- 1/2 tsp dried thyme
- 1/2 tsp dried rosemary
- 2 bay leaves
- 4 carrots, peeled and chopped
- 4 potatoes, peeled and chopped

Directions

1. Season roast with salt and pepper.
2. In a large skillet, heat oil and brown the roast.
3. Transfer to a slow cooker.
4. In the same skillet, sauté onions, mushrooms, and garlic until tender.
5. Add broth, wine (if using), thyme, rosemary, and bay leaves.
6. Pour over the roast in the slow cooker.
7. Cook on low for several hours.
8. Add carrots and potatoes during the last hour.
9. Remove bay leaves before serving.

Fun Facts

Pot roast is a timeless American favorite, ideal for hearty family dinners and special occasions.

4 servings | 350 | 40

Beef Liver and Onions

Slices of beef liver cooked with tender onions. A classic dish for liver lovers.

Ingredients:

- 1 lb beef liver, sliced
- Salt and pepper to taste
- 1/2 cup all-purpose flour
- 2 large onions, thinly sliced
- 1/2 cup beef broth

Directions

1. Season liver with salt and pepper.
2. Dredge liver in flour.
3. In a skillet, cook liver until browned.
4. Remove liver and set aside.
5. In the same skillet, sauté onions until tender.
6. Add beef broth and simmer.
7. Serve liver with onions.

Fun Facts

Beef liver and onions is a classic dish with a devoted following, appreciated for its hearty flavors.

4 servings | 500 | 45

Chicken and Waffles

Crispy fried chicken served on top of fluffy waffles with syrup.
A delightful sweet and savory combo.

Ingredients:

- 4 boneless, skinless chicken breasts
- 2 cups buttermilk
- 2 cups all-purpose flour
- 1 tsp salt
- 1/2 tsp black pepper
- Vegetable oil for frying
- 4 waffles (homemade or store-bought)
- Maple syrup for serving

Directions

1. Pound chicken breasts to an even thickness.
2. Soak in buttermilk.
3. In a shallow dish, combine flour, salt, and pepper.
4. Dredge chicken in the flour mixture.
5. Heat oil in a skillet and fry chicken until golden and cooked through.
6. Serve chicken on top of warm waffles with maple syrup.

Fun Facts

Chicken and waffles is a beloved American dish that combines the crispy and savory with the sweet and fluffy.

4 servings   450   45

Chicken Fried Steak

Tender steak breaded and fried to perfection.
A southern comfort food classic.

Ingredients:

- 4 cube steaks
- Salt and pepper to taste
- 2 cups all-purpose flour
- 1 tsp salt
- 1/2 tsp black pepper
- 1/2 tsp paprika
- 1/4 tsp cayenne pepper
- Vegetable oil for frying
- Gravy for serving (optional)

Directions

1. Season cube steaks with salt and pepper.
2. In a shallow dish, combine flour, salt, pepper, paprika, and cayenne.
3. Dredge cube steaks in the flour mixture.
4. Heat oil in a skillet and fry steaks until golden and cooked through.
5. Serve with gravy if desired.

Fun Facts

Chicken fried steak is a southern comfort food favorite, often served with mashed potatoes and gravy.

Chapter 10:
Global Diner Inspirations

4 servings | 450 | 30

Mexican Breakfast Burrito

A hearty and flavorful breakfast burrito
inspired by Mexican cuisine.
A satisfying start to the day.

Ingredients:

- 4 large eggs
- 1/4 cup milk
- Salt and pepper to taste
- 1/2 cup cooked chorizo sausage
- 1/2 cup diced potatoes, cooked
- 1/4 cup diced onion
- 1/4 cup diced bell pepper
- 1/2 cup shredded cheddar cheese
- 4 large flour tortillas
- Salsa for serving (optional)

Directions

1. In a bowl, whisk eggs, milk, salt, and pepper.
2. In a skillet, scramble eggs with chorizo, potatoes, onion, and bell pepper.
3. Warm tortillas in a dry skillet.
4. Place the egg mixture on each tortilla and top with cheese.
5. Fold into a burrito.
6. Serve with salsa if desired.

Fun Facts

The breakfast burrito is a Tex-Mex invention, combining the heartiness of a breakfast meal with the convenience of a burrito.

4 servings | 400 | 40

Japanese Teriyaki Burger

A juicy burger flavored with sweet and savory teriyaki sauce, inspired by Japanese cuisine. A fusion of flavors.

Ingredients:

- 1 lb ground beef
- 1/4 cup teriyaki sauce
- 4 hamburger buns
- 4 slices pineapple
- 4 lettuce leaves
- 4 slices Swiss cheese
- 4 slices cooked bacon (optional)

Directions

1. Form ground beef into four patties and brush with teriyaki sauce.
2. Grill or cook patties until desired doneness.
3. Grill pineapple slices.
4. Toast buns on the grill.
5. Assemble burgers with lettuce, teriyaki patties, grilled pineapple, Swiss cheese, and bacon if desired.
6. Serve.

Fun Facts

The teriyaki burger combines Japanese and American flavors, offering a unique and delicious twist on the classic burger.

4 servings · 350 · 40

Greek Gyro with Tzatziki

A Greek-inspired gyro filled with tender meat, fresh veggies, and creamy tzatziki sauce. A taste of the Mediterranean.

Ingredients:

- 1 lb boneless lamb or beef, thinly sliced
- 4 pita bread rounds
- 1 cup diced cucumber
- 1/2 cup Greek yogurt
- 2 cloves garlic, minced
- 2 tbsp fresh dill, chopped
- 2 tbsp fresh mint, chopped
- Salt and pepper to taste
- Sliced tomatoes and onions for garnish

Directions

1. Season meat with salt and pepper and grill until cooked.
2. Warm pita bread.
3. In a bowl, combine cucumber, Greek yogurt, garlic, dill, and mint to make tzatziki sauce.
4. Assemble gyros with meat, tzatziki sauce, tomatoes, and onions.
5. Serve.

Fun Facts

The gyro is a popular Greek street food, with origins dating back to the 19th century. It's now enjoyed worldwide.

4 servings   450   45

A classic Italian dish featuring breaded chicken, marinara sauce, and melted cheese. A timeless favorite.

Italian Chicken Parmesan

Ingredients:

- 4 boneless, skinless chicken breasts
- Salt and pepper to taste
- 1 cup all-purpose flour
- 2 large eggs
- 1 cup breadcrumbs
- 1/2 cup grated Parmesan cheese
- 2 cups marinara sauce
- 1 cup shredded mozzarella cheese
- 2 tbsp olive oil
- Fresh basil for garnish

Directions

1. Season chicken with salt and pepper.
2. Dredge chicken in flour, then dip in beaten eggs, and coat with breadcrumbs mixed with Parmesan cheese.
3. Heat olive oil in a skillet and cook chicken until golden and cooked through.
4. Preheat the oven.
5. Place cooked chicken in a baking dish, top with marinara sauce, and mozzarella cheese.
6. Bake until cheese is bubbly.
7. Garnish with fresh basil.

Fun Facts

Chicken Parmesan, also known as "chicken parm" in the United States, is a classic Italian-American dish beloved for its cheesy goodness.

4 servings · 400 kcal · 45

Korean Bibimbap

A Korean rice bowl with a colorful mix of vegetables, marinated meat, and a spicy sauce.
A harmonious blend of flavors.

Ingredients:

- 2 cups cooked white rice
- 1 lb thinly sliced beef (ribeye or sirloin)
- 2 cups julienned carrots
- 2 cups julienned zucchini
- 2 cups bean sprouts
- 2 cups sliced shiitake mushrooms
- 4 large eggs
- 4 tbsp gochujang (Korean red pepper paste)
- 2 tbsp soy sauce
- 2 tbsp sesame oil
- 1 tsp sugar
- 4 cloves garlic, minced
- 2 tsp vegetable oil

Directions

1. In a bowl, mix sliced beef with soy sauce, sesame oil, sugar, and garlic.
2. In a hot skillet, cook the marinated beef until done.
3. In the same skillet, add vegetable oil and stir-fry each vegetable separately.
4. In another skillet, fry eggs sunny-side up.
5. Assemble bibimbap bowls with rice, beef, and a variety of vegetables.
6. Top with a fried egg and a dollop of gochujang.
7. Mix everything together before eating.

Fun Facts

Bibimbap is a popular Korean dish known for its vibrant colors and dynamic flavors. It's often served in a hot stone bowl.

4 servings   350   30

French Croque Monsieur

A French grilled ham and cheese sandwich, smothered in béchamel sauce.
A decadent delight.

Ingredients:

- 8 slices of white bread
- 8 slices of ham
- 8 slices of Gruyère or Swiss cheese
- 4 tbsp butter
- 1/4 cup all-purpose flour
- 2 cups milk
- Salt, pepper, and nutmeg to taste

Directions

1. Preheat the oven.
2. Make a béchamel sauce: In a saucepan, melt butter, add flour, and cook for a few minutes.
3. Gradually whisk in milk and cook until thickened.
4. Season with salt, pepper, and a pinch of nutmeg.
5. Assemble sandwiches with ham and cheese.
6. Spread a layer of béchamel sauce on top of each sandwich.
7. Bake until golden and bubbly.

Fun Facts

The Croque Monsieur is a beloved French sandwich that combines the simplicity of ham and cheese with the elegance of béchamel sauce.

4 servings   400   30

Cuban Cubano Sandwich

A Cuban sandwich filled with roasted pork, ham, pickles, and mustard.
A fusion of flavors.

Ingredients:

- 1 Cuban bread loaf or baguette
- 1/2 lb roasted pork, thinly sliced
- 1/2 lb ham, thinly sliced
- 1/2 cup dill pickles, sliced
- 1/4 cup yellow mustard
- 4 slices Swiss cheese

Directions

1. Preheat a sandwich press or grill.
2. Slice the bread in half and spread mustard on both sides.
3. Layer the roasted pork, ham, Swiss cheese, and pickles.
4. Close the sandwich and press or grill until the bread is crispy and the cheese is melted.
5. Slice and serve.

Fun Facts

The Cubano sandwich is a Cuban-American creation, influenced by the flavors of both Cuban and American cuisines.

4 servings   350   60

Indian Tandoori Chicken

Tandoori chicken, marinated in yogurt and spices, and cooked to perfection in a tandoor or oven.
A taste of India.

Ingredients:

- 4 bone-in chicken thighs
- 1 cup plain yogurt
- 2 tbsp tandoori spice blend
- 2 cloves garlic, minced
- 2-inch piece of ginger, grated
- Juice of 1 lemon
- Salt to taste
- Cilantro for garnish

Directions

1. In a bowl, combine yogurt, tandoori spice blend, garlic, ginger, lemon juice, and salt.
2. Make deep cuts in the chicken thighs and coat them with the marinade.
3. Marinate for at least 2 hours, or overnight for best results.
4. Preheat a grill or oven to high heat.
5. Grill or bake the chicken until fully cooked.
6. Garnish with cilantro and serve.

Fun Facts

Tandoori chicken is a popular Indian dish known for its vibrant red color and bold flavors, often cooked in a tandoor oven.

4 servings   400   45

Tex-Mex Enchiladas

Enchiladas with a Tex-Mex twist, filled with seasoned meat, cheese, and smothered in red sauce.
A south-of-the-border delight.

Ingredients:

- 1 lb ground beef or turkey
- 1 small onion, chopped
- 2 cups shredded cheddar cheese
- 8 corn tortillas
- 2 cups red enchilada sauce
- Sour cream and chopped cilantro for garnish (optional)

Directions

1. Preheat the oven.
2. In a skillet, cook meat and onions until browned.
3. Warm tortillas.
4. Fill each tortilla with meat and cheese, roll, and place seam-side down in a baking dish.
5. Pour enchilada sauce over the top.
6. Bake until bubbly and cheese is melted.
7. Garnish with sour cream and cilantro if desired.

Fun Facts

Tex-Mex enchiladas combine the flavors of Mexico and the southwestern United States, creating a delicious fusion.

4 servings | 400 | 30

Thai Peanut Noodles

A Thai-inspired dish featuring tender noodles in a rich and creamy peanut sauce. A burst of Asian flavors.

Ingredients:

- 8 oz rice noodles
- 1/2 cup peanut butter
- 1/4 cup soy sauce
- 1/4 cup lime juice
- 2 tbsp honey
- 1 clove garlic, minced
- 1/4 cup chopped cilantro
- 1/4 cup chopped peanuts
- Sliced green onions for garnish

Directions

1. Cook rice noodles according to package instructions.
2. In a bowl, whisk together peanut butter, soy sauce, lime juice, honey, and garlic to make the sauce.
3. Toss cooked noodles in the peanut sauce.
4. Garnish with cilantro, peanuts, and sliced green onions.
5. Serve.

Fun Facts

Thai peanut noodles offer a delightful mix of sweet, savory, and spicy flavors, a hallmark of Thai cuisine.

Chapter 11:
Diner Drinks and Shakes

2 servings | 350 | 10

Classic Chocolate Milkshake

A timeless and indulgent chocolate milkshake. A sweet and creamy classic.

Ingredients:

- 2 cups vanilla ice cream
- 1/2 cup whole milk
- 1/4 cup chocolate syrup
- Whipped cream for garnish (optional)
- Maraschino cherry for garnish (optional)

Directions

1. In a blender, combine ice cream, milk, and chocolate syrup.
2. Blend until smooth and creamy.
3. Pour into glasses.
4. Top with whipped cream and a cherry if desired.

Fun Facts

The chocolate milkshake is an American classic, enjoyed in diners and ice cream parlors for generations.

2 servings | 200 | 5

Root Beer Float

A simple and delightful combination of root beer and vanilla ice cream.
A fizzy and sweet treat.

Ingredients:

- 2 scoops vanilla ice cream
- 2 cups root beer
- Whipped cream for garnish (optional)
- Maraschino cherry for garnish (optional)

Directions

1. Place a scoop of vanilla ice cream in each glass.
2. Slowly pour root beer over the ice cream.
3. Top with whipped cream and a cherry if desired.
4. Serve with a straw and a long spoon.

Fun Facts

The root beer float is a classic American dessert beverage, often enjoyed in soda fountains and diners.

2 servings | 250 | 5

Easy

Cream Soda

A refreshing and effervescent cream soda with a hint of vanilla.
A sweet and bubbly delight.

Ingredients:

- 2 cups club soda
- 1/2 cup heavy cream
- 1/4 cup vanilla syrup
- Ice cubes
- Whipped cream for garnish (optional)
- Maraschino cherry for garnish (optional)

Directions

1. Fill glasses with ice cubes.
2. In each glass, combine club soda, heavy cream, and vanilla syrup.
3. Stir gently.
4. Top with whipped cream and a cherry if desired.
5. Serve with a straw.

Fun Facts

Cream soda is a classic carbonated soft drink with a creamy and sweet vanilla flavor.

2 servings | 120 | 5

Freshly Squeezed Orange Juice

A simple and refreshing drink made from freshly squeezed oranges.
A burst of citrus flavor.

Ingredients:

- 4 large oranges, freshly squeezed
- Ice cubes
- Orange slices for garnish (optional)

Directions

1. Squeeze the juice from the oranges.
2. Fill glasses with ice cubes.
3. Pour the freshly squeezed orange juice into the glasses.
4. Garnish with orange slices if desired.
5. Serve immediately.

Fun Facts

Freshly squeezed orange juice is a natural and vitamin-packed beverage, perfect for a quick burst of energy.

2 servings   200   5

Chocolate Egg Cream

An old-school New York classic, this beverage combines milk, chocolate syrup, and seltzer. A delightful and frothy drink.

Ingredients:

- 1/2 cup whole milk
- 2 tbsp chocolate syrup
- 1/2 cup seltzer water

Directions

1. In a glass, combine milk and chocolate syrup.
2. Stir well to combine.
3. Slowly pour in seltzer water.
4. Stir gently until frothy.
5. Serve immediately.

Fun Facts

The chocolate egg cream is a classic New York City drink, despite containing neither eggs nor cream.

2 servings   400   10

Classic Malted Milkshake

A malted milkshake with a touch of nostalgia. Creamy, malty, and irresistible.

Ingredients:

- 2 cups vanilla ice cream
- 1/2 cup whole milk
- 2 tbsp malted milk powder
- Whipped cream for garnish (optional)
- Maraschino cherry for garnish (optional)

Directions

1. In a blender, combine ice cream, milk, and malted milk powder.
2. Blend until smooth and creamy.
3. Pour into glasses.
4. Top with whipped cream and a cherry if desired.

Fun Facts

The malted milkshake is a classic diner favorite, featuring the unique flavor of malted milk powder.

2 servings | 5 | 5

Diner Coffee

A simple cup of diner-style coffee, dark and aromatic.
A comforting caffeine boost.

Ingredients:

- 2 cups freshly brewed coffee
- Cream and sugar to taste (optional)

Directions

1. Brew coffee to your preferred strength.
2. Add cream and sugar to taste if desired.
3. Stir and serve hot.

Fun Facts

Diner coffee is a staple in diners across the country, providing a warm and comforting start to the day.

2 servings   200   5

Old-Fashioned Cherry Coke

A classic soda fountain favorite, combining cola with cherry syrup.
A sweet and tangy treat.

Ingredients:

- 2 cups cola (e.g., Coca-Cola)
- 2 tbsp cherry syrup
- Ice cubes
- Maraschino cherry for garnish (optional)

Directions

1. Fill glasses with ice cubes.
2. In each glass, combine cola and cherry syrup.
3. Stir gently.
4. Garnish with a maraschino cherry if desired.
5. Serve with a straw.

Fun Facts

Cherry Coke is a beloved soda flavor, known for its delightful combination of cola and cherry.

2 servings   150   10

Classic Diner Lemonade

A simple and refreshing lemonade, sweet and tangy.
A thirst-quenching classic.

Ingredients:

- 2 large lemons, freshly squeezed
- 1/2 cup granulated sugar
- 2 cups water
- Ice cubes
- Lemon slices for garnish (optional)

Directions

1. Squeeze the juice from the lemons.
2. In a pitcher, combine lemon juice, sugar, and water.
3. Stir until sugar is dissolved.
4. Fill glasses with ice cubes.
5. Pour the lemonade over the ice.
6. Garnish with lemon slices if desired.
7. Serve chilled.

Fun Facts

Classic diner lemonade is a timeless thirst quencher, perfect for a hot summer day or any time you need a refreshing sip.

2 servings | 100 | 10

A classic combination of iced tea and lemonade.
A refreshing and balanced drink.

Arnold Palmer

Ingredients:

- 1 cup freshly brewed iced tea
- 1 cup classic diner lemonade (see previous recipe)
- Ice cubes
- Lemon slices for garnish (optional)

Directions

1. Brew iced tea and let it cool.
2. In a glass, combine equal parts iced tea and classic diner lemonade.
3. Add ice cubes.
4. Garnish with lemon slices if desired.
5. Serve with a straw.

Fun Facts

The Arnold Palmer, named after the legendary golfer, is a perfect blend of iced tea and lemonade, offering the best of both worlds.

We have a small favor to ask

As we savor the last bites of our diner classics journey through the "Best of Diner Classics Cookbook: A Taste of Nostalgia - 100+ Best Copycat Classic American Dinners Recipes," I want to share a heartfelt request.

Reviews, my fellow diners-at-heart, are like the comforting hum of a diner on a Sunday morning—warm, essential, and deeply appreciated. For a small publisher like us, they are the comforting booth in the corner that keeps us going.

If you could spare a moment, please revisit the platform where you discovered this taste of nostalgia—whether it's an app or an online marketplace. There, like the familiar clink of a coffee mug against a saucer, you'll find the review button. We would be genuinely grateful if you could grace us with your honest rating and a brief, flavorful sentence capturing your diner classics experience.

Every review is a slice of apple pie for us. They're the sizzle of bacon on a griddle, making our cookbook truly reminiscent of the classic diner experience. In the spirit of openness, should you stumble upon a minor hiccup within these pages, please know we've manned the grill with dedication. We're not infallible, and, much like the occasional wobble in a diner stool, small mistakes can happen. We hope you can relish the overall diner experience despite these minor imperfections.

Your support, conveyed through a review, is like the perfect pairing of pancakes and syrup—it completes the meal and inspires us to keep serving up delightful diner classics. So, please, take a moment, and let your words be the extra sprinkle of powdered sugar on our diner masterpiece.

We deeply appreciate your time, your discerning palate, and your love for the timeless world of diner classics. After all, this cookbook isn't just about recipes; it's about celebrating the nostalgia of classic American dinners with fellow diner aficionados. With sincere gratitude and a toast to a perfectly brewed cup of coffee, we eagerly await your feedback. May your future diner experiences be filled with the warmth and flavor of a true classic American meal!